CW00995964

Original title:
Echoes of Edifices

Author: Clement Portlander
ISBN HARDBACK: 978-9916-88-100-2
ISBN PAPERBACK: 978-9916-88-101-9

Murmurs from the Marble

In shadows cast by ancient stone,
Whispers echo of the past alone.
Each chisel strike tells tales untold,
Silent secrets in the marble hold.

Softly flows the evening light,
Highlighting curves both bold and slight.
As time drapes its gentle veil,
These murmurs dance, a timeless trail.

Tales of Towering Temples

Inspire tall, their spires ascend,
Stories etched where stone and sky blend.
Each column stands, a sentinel wise,
Guarding dreams that touch the skies.

Whispers of prayers wane and rise,
Chanting hope beneath boundless skies.
In every crack, a history lies,
Tales of faith that never dies.

The Architecture of Memory

Within the walls of heart and mind,
Lay blueprints of the past we find.
Each moment framed, an intricate design,
Crafted by time, both cruel and kind.

Rooms of laughter, halls of tears,
Echoes of joy, shadows of fears.
Through time's corridors we wistfully roam,
Building bridges to a long-lost home.

Fragments of Time in the Breeze

As whispers travel on the air,
They carry fragments, light as prayer.
Which flutter softly, dance and weave,
In the golden hours we perceive.

Memories drift like autumn leaves,
In gentle sways, the heart believes.
Time's tapestry, so rich, so vast,
We gather moments, hold them fast.

Crescendo of the Colonnade

Whispers of winds within the stone,
A symphony played for the lone.
Each pillar stands tall and proud,
Echoing tales to the crowd.

Shadows dance under moonlit light,
Framing thoughts in the quiet night.
Nature's music, soft yet grand,
Guides the hearts that understand.

Latticed Dreams in the Attic

Dusty beams hold secrets untold,
Frayed edges of dreams, lost but bold.
Curtains sway in gentle sighs,
Cocooned beneath the watchful skies.

Whispers of laughter linger still,
Fleeting moments, time can't kill.
In the shadows, stories grow,
Waiting for someone to know.

Histories Carved in the Earth

Footprints left on paths of clay,
Each one tells a tale today.
Rivers carve the ancient lore,
Woven deep at the earth's core.

Time stands still, while tales unfold,
Nature's canvas, bold and cold.
Echoes of life, lost and found,
In every wrinkle of the ground.

Resonant Remains on the Horizon

Silhouettes of dreams drift high,
Where the land kisses the sky.
Every stone a memory stirs,
Tales of life that silence blurs.

Waves of time roll in and out,
Carrying whispers, softly shout.
Though the past may fade away,
Its essence here will always stay.

The Soundtrack of Stony Silence

In the hush of the night, shadows creep,
Whispers echo where secrets sleep.
A melody forged in quieted stone,
Every silence sings, though we stand alone.

Moonlight dances on paths we tread,
Thoughts linger softly, words left unsaid.
The weight of absence, a song so profound,
In the stony silence, lost voices abound.

Tides of Time in Tall Towers

High above in towers bold,
Stories of time quietly unfold.
Waves of history crash and churn,
Lessons lost, but we yearn to learn.

Underneath the watchful skies,
Each tick of the clock, a silent guise.
Moments drift like clouds in flight,
In the tall towers, day turns to night.

Embers of the Erected

In the ruins where dreams have burned,
Embers of hope shimmer and turned.
Structures tall, now mere silhouettes,
Echoes of laughter, the heart forgets.

Through the ashes, new blooms arise,
Whispers of promise beneath the skies.
In every scar, strength is reflected,
From the embers, life is resurrected.

Fractured Reflections in Glass

Shattered fragments on the floor,
Stories of lives that were once more.
Each piece a glimpse of what once was,
In the cracks, there lies a pause.

Through a window, the world may change,
Beauty found in what feels strange.
Reflections ripple like the past,
In fractured glass, memories cast.

Clear as Day

The sun breaks through, a gentle glow,
Casting shadows that dance below.
Whispers of warmth in the cool of morn,
A world reborn, bright and adorned.

Birds take flight, a joyful choir,
Sky painted blue, heart lifting higher.
Each moment shines with purpose and grace,
Living in truth, in time and space.

Lost in Dusk

The sky ignites in hues of fire,
As day gives way to night's desire.
Stars awaken, one by one,
Lost in dusk, the day's undone.

Shadows stretch, like stories told,
In the hush of twilight, secrets unfold.
The moon's soft light, a guiding hand,
Lost in dusk, where dreams can stand.

Threads Woven in Concrete

Amidst the steel and the stone,
Life's tapestry is gently sown.
A child's laughter, echoes clear,
Threads of memory we hold dear.

In every crack, a story waits,
In whispered secrets, life narrates.
Through busy streets, connections grow,
Threads woven in time, we all know.

Where Past Meets Present

In the quiet of an old town square,
Time stands still, memories share.
Footprints linger, paths once trod,
Where past meets present, silence nods.

Stories woven in every wall,
Echoes of laughter, a distant call.
In the hearts of those who stay,
Where past meets present, night meets day.

The Weight of What Remains

In the attic dust, old dreams reside,
Ghosts of laughter, too hard to hide.
Photographs fade, but feelings stay,
The weight of what remains in gray.

Time may pass, but love endures,
Held in moments, memories pure.
Through every loss, we find a sign,
The weight of what remains is divine.

Echoing Heartbeats of History

In ancient halls where whispers dwell,
Old stories weave their timeless spell.
Each echo carries tales of yore,
Of battles fought, of love, and more.

The walls remember every tear,
The laughter, joy, the silent fear.
Through dust-laden paths, time stands still,
An endless dance, a fated will.

Footsteps trace the lives once led,
In shadows where the brave have tread.
Their heartbeats linger, soft and low,
As history's river ceaseless flows.

The weight of ages on the air,
In every breath, a solemn prayer.
We are but echoes, fleeting, brief,
In the grand tapestry of belief.

The Sigh of the Weathered Roof

Beneath the eaves where time has passed,
A weary roof, its memories cast.
Each shingle whispers tales of rain,
Of storms that danced, of quiet pain.

The wind caresses with gentle grace,
As shadows flicker, time's embrace.
In cracked wood grain, the stories lie,
Of dreams that bloomed, and those that die.

A refuge made of years gone by,
While seasons change, the heart does sigh.
In twilight's glow, the silence speaks,
Of laughter lost, of weary weeks.

Yet still it stands, though weathered, worn,
A shelter where hope is gently born.
In every creak, a life retold,
A testament to love, at bold.

Phantoms Beneath the Portico

In twilight's hue, shadows expand,
Where phantoms dance through moonlit land.
The portico, a sacred place,
Holds secrets close in soft embrace.

Whispers linger, soft as sighs,
Of hidden dreams and silent cries.
Beneath the arch where history waits,
The past entwines, and fate creates.

Figures dimmed by the veil of time,
Each step recounts a solemn rhyme.
In the soft glow of fading light,
The phantoms come to claim the night.

A dance of shadows, fleeting, swift,
In haunting echoes, memories lift.
They wander still, though years have flown,
In every heart, they find a home.

The Silent Watch of Stately Spires

In cities grand, where dreams arise,
The spires stand with watchful eyes.
Their shadows stretch on cobbled streets,
Guarding tales where past and future meets.

Above the hustle, calm and bold,
They witness stories yet untold.
Through storm and sun, they keep their place,
A steadfast watch, a timeless grace.

Each stone, a page, of history's tome,
In whispered winds, they call us home.
Their silent vigil, strong and sure,
Marks every heart that dares endure.

In twilight's glow, their peaks aglow,
Remind us all how far we go.
Through trials faced, and dreams embraced,
The spires watch, with love interlaced.

Resonance of Ruins

Whispers linger in the stones,
Echoes of what once was home.
Shadows stretch across the ground,
Time's embrace, forever bound.

Crumbled walls tell tales untold,
Secrets of the brave and bold.
Nature weaves her gentle thread,
In every crack, where dreams have fled.

Sunlight filters through decay,
A haunting dance of light and gray.
In silence, history is revealed,
A sacred ground, where hearts once healed.

Silhouettes Beneath the Sky

Figures cast in twilight's glow,
Stories etched in each shadow.
The horizon whispers soft and low,
As the stars begin to show.

Gentle winds stir through the night,
Carrying echoes of past flight.
Beneath the vast and endless dome,
Hearts find solace, a sense of home.

Silent wishes float on air,
Yearnings shared without a care.
In shadows' depths, we come alive,
As silhouettes, we thrive and strive.

Soft Footfalls on Ancient Steps

Steps worn down by time's embrace,
Each footfall finds a special place.
Whispers of those who came before,
Echo softly through the core.

Moss-clad stones know every tread,
Memories linger, long since dead.
The path unfolds with every turn,
Ancient wisdom waits to learn.

In whispers of the evening mist,
We feel the pulses of the past.
Time entwines in every stride,
On ancient steps, our dreams abide.

Remnants of a Silent Past

In corners dark, the echoes fade,
Memories lost in the glade.
Faded pages softly sigh,
Tales of love that passed them by.

Curtains drawn, a stillness reigns,
Ghostly laughter, distant pains.
Fragments of life, like autumn leaves,
In quiet corners, the heart believes.

Dust swirls gently in the light,
A reminder of the night.
Time recedes, a gentle wave,
In remnants, we find the brave.

Questioning the Quiet of Quoins

In corners where shadows blend,
A whisper of history ascends.
Silent echoes mark the stone,
Boundless stories left alone.

Questioning the stillness here,
Each crack a tale, sharp and clear.
Quoins stand proud, yet they bend,
Holding secrets without end.

Walls have watched the ages pass,
In their grip, the moments last.
Time drapes quiet on their face,
Memories linger in this space.

Do these stones remember me?
Or are they lost in reverie?
In the hush, a voice, a sigh,
Quoins remind me to ask why.

Footfalls on the Fabric of Time

Step by step on threads so fine,
Each footfall weaves a story line.
From past to present, shadows play,
In the fabric of time, dreams sway.

Echoes linger from days gone by,
Whispers carry like a sigh.
Moments stitched with care and grace,
Footfalls mark this sacred space.

Every path a tale to tell,
Of laughter, love, of rise and fell.
The fabric stretches, bends, and folds,
In every stitch, a life unfolds.

Bearing witness to the years,
Threads entwined with hopes and fears.
Time dances softly, slow or fast,
Footfalls linger, shadows cast.

Shades of Stories in Stone

Captured shadows on the wall,
Carved in stone, they seem to call.
Whispers painted with a brush,
In shades of gray, a silent hush.

Each crevice holds a secret tight,
In dim-lit corners, sparks ignite.
Stories flourish out of view,
In subtle tones, both old and new.

The stone remembers every fable,
Crafted dreams upon the table.
A tapestry of light and dark,
Within the gray, a sacred spark.

The past reflects in muted hues,
Each story threading through the blues.
In shades of stories, truth is sown,
The heart of stone is never alone.

Memory's Mosaic in the Masons

In each brick, a line of thought,
Memories layered, battles fought.
Masons' hands, with care, they place,
Creating time's enduring grace.

Fragments join to form a whole,
In every gap, a lost soul.
History's whispers in the seams,
A mosaic born of hopes and dreams.

Patterns weave through time and space,
In this art, we find our place.
Every stone a voice, a song,
In memory's grip, we all belong.

As the light falls, stories rise,
In the shadows, the truth lies.
A tapestry of lives embraced,
Memory's mosaic, time's own grace.

The Vault of Vertical Visions

In towers where dreams ascend,
Visions of the future blend.
Glass and steel touch the sky,
Echoes of hopes gone by.

Streets alive with whispered tales,
Mirrored paths where spirit sails.
Eyes upturned, souls collide,
In shadows where secrets hide.

Arquitects of our own fate,
Sketching life at a fast rate.
Each floor holds a memory,
Time suspended, endlessly.

At night the city breathes light,
A symphony of vibrant sights.
In the vault of dreams we soar,
Forever longing for more.

The Afterglow of Urban Memory

Beneath the streetlamps' warm gaze,
The city hums in a golden haze.
Footprints linger on cobblestones,
Whispers of life in muted tones.

Windows frame the dusk's embrace,
Ghosts of laughter, fading grace.
Every corner, every block,
Holds stories in a ticking clock.

In alleys where shadows play,
Memories wander, drift away.
Graffiti blooms, a canvas bright,
Capturing echoes of the night.

As stars puncture the deepening sky,
Time tells tales that never die.
Urban dreams, like fireflies glow,
In the afterglow, we have to know.

Past Lives Carved in the Clay

Hands mold history with soft care,
Ancient echoes linger in the air.
Figures rise from earth and dust,
Each shape holds secrets we trust.

Fossils of lives, a silent throng,
Whispered sagas, both short and long.
Roots entwined in tales of old,
In every crack, a story told.

Molded faces from times gone by,
Eyes that once gazed at the sky.
Each shard reflects a heartbeat's pulse,
In the clay, our dreams convulse.

Imprints left by hands divine,
Ink of time, a sacred line.
In this earth, we find our way,
Past lives carved, forever stay.

What Remains in the Ruin

Stone and silence stand as one,
Memories of a life once spun.
What remains in crumbling walls,
Are whispers of the past's soft calls.

Beneath the rubble, a heartbeat thuds,
Ghostly laughter, the scent of blood.
Roots break through in grand designs,
Nature reclaiming what's defined.

In twilight's glow, shadows dance,
Each fragment holds a fleeting chance.
History etched in every line,
What remains becomes divine.

Through cracked façades, stories leak,
The broken speak, the ruins seek.
In what's left, we find our grace,
In the ruin's touch, we face our place.

Histories etched in Dust

In corners where the shadows creep,
The tales of old begin to seep.
Dusty tomes and whispered sighs,
Echoes trapped beneath the skies.

Fingers trace the stories bold,
Of lives once lived, of dreams retold.
Every grain a memory lost,
A testament to paths we've crossed.

Time weaves threads in muted hues,
Binding futures, shaping views.
Through history's lens, we look past,
Finding wisdom in the vast.

So gather round, let voices rise,
In dusty halls where truth belies.
For every story, every trust,
Lives forever in the dust.

Footsteps on Faded Floors

Upon the wood, the echoes play,
Of footsteps from another day.
In whispers soft, the memories throng,
Each creak a note in a silent song.

Once vibrant souls filled every room,
Now shadows linger, a muted gloom.
Faded paths where laughter soared,
In dreams they dance, forever adored.

Dust motes float in beams of light,
Marking time in the soft twilight.
Each footfall tells a tale anew,
Of love and loss we must pursue.

So take a step, feel the past's embrace,
In faded floors, find your place.
With every move, let the stories soar,
In the echoes of those who walked before.

The Soul of a Dying Column

Stalwart stand the aging stones,
Whispers rise in weary tones.
Each crack a tale of time and strife,
The silent witness of a life.

Once proud and tall, a beacon bright,
Now shadows cloak its fading light.
The winds of change begin to call,
Yet still it stands, enduring all.

Moss and ivy weave their dreams,
As nature's hand gently redeems.
In every fissure, secrets dwell,
The soul of history, cast in spell.

As twilight dims the ancient frame,
The column sighs, yet bears no shame.
For in its heart, the echoes stay,
A testament to yesterday.

Secrets Held in the Hearth

In the heart of every home,
Where whispered tales and embers roam.
The hearth, a guardian of the past,
Holds secrets in its warmth steadfast.

Crackling flames and soothing light,
Reveal the shadows of the night.
Gathered close, the stories weave,
Of dreams, of hopes, of hearts that grieve.

From ancient times to futures bright,
The hearth's embrace feels just right.
In every flicker, a memory sparked,
A flame of love forever marked.

So sit awhile, let silence reign,
In the hearth, feel joy and pain.
For in this space, where echoes dwell,
Are secrets kept, the stories tell.

Stories Carved in Granite

In shadows deep, where whispers dwell,
Stone speaks tales, where echoes swell.
Each chisel mark, a history's breath,
Carved in silence, transcending death.

Mighty towers reach for the sky,
Their stories linger, as dreams fly.
Upon the heart of ancient stone,
Lie legends lost, now overgrown.

Through weathered walls, the past unfolds,
A testament to the brave and bold.
Granite giants hold the night,
Guarding secrets, hidden from sight.

Visions entwined, they stand their ground,
In every crevice, history's found.
Time stands still in their embrace,
Stories carved, forever trace.

The Breath of Time-Touched Beams

Sunlight dances, beams of gold,
Whispers of warmth, stories told.
In quiet corners, memories play,
The breath of time, a fleeting ray.

Each timber sighs with age and grace,
Holding moments, a sacred space.
Through weathered knots and grainy lines,
Resilience wove in nature's designs.

Shadowed halls where laughter rang,
Echoes linger, sweetly sang.
Time-touched beams, a soft embrace,
Cradle dreams in a timeless trace.

With every dawn, the light anew,
Painted hues of an unseen view.
In the pulse of life, we find our theme,
The breath of time, a living dream.

Lullabies of Lonesome Lintels

Underneath the moon's soft gaze,
Lies a home in a silvery haze.
Lonesome lintels, shadows cast,
Sing lullabies of a distant past.

Faded whispers, creaks of wood,
Tell of love and laughter, good.
In the stillness, their stories weave,
A tapestry that won't deceive.

Gently swaying in a gentle breeze,
Carrying dreams with utmost ease.
Lullabies echo through the night,
Guarding hearts till morning light.

As dawn breaks, shadows fade,
Hope rekindled, foundations laid.
Lonesome lintels hold the key,
To voices lost in history.

Traces of the Builders' Legacy

Hands that crafted, dreams in stone,
Traces linger, never alone.
With each brick laid, a promise made,
A legacy of love displayed.

The builders' sweat upon the ground,
In every corner, stories found.
From towering arches to winding stairs,
Their purpose lives, etched in prayers.

Through storms and time, their tales remain,
Resilient spirits, born of pain.
Crafted visions, bold and wide,
In the heart of stone, they bide.

Echoes of those who came before,
Unlock the dreams behind each door.
In silent strength, their mark we see,
Traces of a shared legacy.

Stories Stained by Sunlight

Once upon a dream so bright,
Colors danced in morning light,
Whispers of the tales untold,
In shadows deep, the warmth behold.

Memories etched on golden leaves,
Gentle sighs the heart believes,
Sunlight spills on paths we tread,
In every moment, words are spread.

Where laughter rings and echoes play,
Time unfolds in bright array,
Stories whispered by the breeze,
In sunlight's arms, the soul finds ease.

With every heartbeat, tales revive,
In daylight's glow, the past alive,
Stained by joy, the sunlit hue,
In stories shared, we find what's true.

The Weight of Lost Heights

Mountains stand with shadows cast,
Echoes of a flight so fast,
Memories cling to rugged stone,
A silent cry, a heartsick moan.

Once we soared on wings of dreams,
Now the valley's silence screams,
The peaks we climbed, now far away,
In heavy hearts, the skies turn gray.

Each step down is laced with pain,
The weight of loss, like falling rain,
Yet through the tears, we find our way,
Towards the dawn of a brighter day.

The heights we reach, and those we mourn,
In every loss, a life reborn,
With every struggle, strength made clear,
In love's embrace, we conquer fear.

Palaces of Wind and Wonder

Amidst the clouds, where dreams take flight,
Palaces gleam in the soft moonlight,
Whispers of magic fill the air,
In every corner, wonders flare.

Towers rise with the songs of the breeze,
Dancing shadows in the rustling trees,
Mirrors of starlight, reflections of time,
In these halls, the heart will climb.

Echoes of laughter, ancient and wise,
In every gaze, the cosmos lies,
Wonders wrapped in the fabric of night,
In palaces built on dreams so bright.

From heights unknown, to lands afar,
Guided gently by each shining star,
In wind's embrace, we find our way,
Through palaces of light, forever stay.

Breaths of the Old

Ancient trees with stories weave,
In creaking branches, whispers leave,
Breaths of the old, in silence speak,
Time's gentle touch on a weathered cheek.

Roots entangled in tales of yore,
Each rustling leaf, a memory's door,
Moments captured in the bark's embrace,
In every wrinkle, a time-worn grace.

Seasons shift, yet wisdom stays,
In the twilight glow of fading days,
Breaths of the old, a guiding light,
In shadows deep, they hold us tight.

Through ages past, their spirits flow,
In every breath, a love we know,
In nature's arms, we stand so bold,
Embraced forever in breaths of the old.

Song of the Steepled Shadows

Beneath the steeple's watchful eye,
Whispers drift where shadows lie.
Echoes play on quiet stones,
Carved in time, like ancient bones.

In twilight's glow, they dance and sway,
Silent songs of yesterday.
Each hush a tale, each breath a sigh,
In the heart where dreams comply.

As moonlight bathes the cobbled street,
The shadows gather, soft and sweet.
Their fleeting forms, a phantom's grace,
In the stillness, time's embrace.

A serenade to those who roam,
Through echoing nights, they find their home.
With every note, the past revives,
In the music, the spirit thrives.

Glimmers of the Graveled Paths

Along the paths of gravel laid,
Where sunlight dances, softly played.
Each step, a glimmer, bright and fair,
Whispers of stories linger there.

In rustling leaves, the secrets sigh,
A gentle breeze that wanders by.
The crunch of stones beneath the tread,
Guides weary souls to dreams ahead.

When twilight falls and shadows stretch,
The glimmers fade, yet still they fetch.
The memories of what has been,
In every path, the heart's akin.

With every turn, new sights appear,
A tapestry of joy and fear.
As night descends, the stars ignite,
The paths remembered, pure delight.

Fleeting Echoes Amongst the Eaves

Amidst the eaves where silence waits,
Fleeting echoes contemplate fates.
They brush the rafters, soft and low,
Stories gathered, long ago.

With every gust, a whisper flies,
Carrying past beneath the skies.
In creaking wood, the time discloses,
The scent of rain, the bloom of roses.

Ghostly murmurs in the night,
Memories cloaked in silver light.
They weave through darkness, soft and vague,
In corners where the shadows plague.

Yet in that space, a warmth persists,
A gentle touch within the mist.
For every echo left unspoken,
Holds the heart's string, never broken.

Dawn in Dusty Dormers

Dawn peeks through the dusty panes,
A golden light that softly reigns.
In dormers high, where dreams have lain,
The world awakens, free from chains.

With every ray, the shadows flee,
Revealing all that's meant to be.
In gentle hues, the morning breaks,
The heart rejoices, hope awakes.

The whispers of the night undone,
As day begins, the battles won.
Through dusty dormers, life's embrace,
Unfurls anew, a tender grace.

So let the dawn, in silence wrapped,
Kiss dreams to life, and fears untapped.
With open arms, we greet the day,
In golden light, we find our way.

Tales Suspended in the Vault

In shadows deep where secrets lie,
Ancient stories start to cry.
Whispers echo through the night,
Hearts aflame with lost delight.

Beneath the stone, the shadows crawl,
Memories dance within the hall.
Each breath holds a tale untold,
Time's embrace, a grip so bold.

Flickering flames weave through the air,
Casting forms of those who dare.
Echoes linger, soft and sweet,
Threads of fate where shadows meet.

In the vault, the tales reside,
In hushed tones, they bide their time.
Unraveling slowly, a precious thread,
Binding hearts, both lost and led.

Reflections in the Ruined Glass

Shattered pieces, dreams forlorn,
Glimmers catch the light of morn.
In the fragments, stories weave,
Lives once lived, now take their leave.

The whispers call from shades of gray,
In every shard, a dance of day.
Memory's breath upon the pane,
A tapestry born from the pain.

Glimmers of hope in sorrow's face,
In brokenness, we find our place.
Reflections linger, soft and clear,
Haunting whispers we long to hear.

Through fractured dreams, the past will roam,
A journey of the heart, a home.
In every crack, a story lies,
In ruined glass, our spirit flies.

Whispers in the Stone

Beneath the earth, in silence bides,
A tapestry where history hides.
Stones bear witness, tales of old,
Secrets shelter, brave and bold.

Softly echoes, footfalls pass,
Through ancient halls of time's vast glass.
Each whisper, like the softest sigh,
Invokes the shadows roaming by.

Moss-covered tales in twilight dim,
Dance on the edges, softly skim.
Roots entwined with every lore,
Binding nature and the core.

As night's curtain draws so near,
Whispers rise, a song to hear.
In every stone, a heartbeats' tone,
A timeless verse, forever grown.

Shadows of Forgotten Walls

In quiet corners, shadows loom,
Embraced by walls of dust and gloom.
Faded echoes whisper past,
Memories lingering, shadows cast.

Time's soft hand caresses stone,
Each crack and crevice sings alone.
A symphony of ages gone,
In muted tones, the heart's drawn.

Sunbeams trace the history's line,
A dance through shadows, so divine.
Walls that once held laughter's sound,
Now breathe silence, tightly bound.

Yet hope remains in every fold,
In forgotten walls, new tales unfold.
Where shadows dwell in colors pale,
Stories whisper on the gale.

The Pulse of Weathered Granite

In the depths of ancient stone,
Whispers of time are deftly sown.
Beneath the weight of every year,
Nature's tales are crystal clear.

Veins of quartz like rivers flow,
Silent witness to fire's glow.
Moss and lichen cling with grace,
Embracing time's unyielding pace.

Echoes dance on crests and ledges,
Stalwart guardians of past pledges.
The pulse beneath, a steady beat,
In weathered granite, life's heartbeat.

Carved by storms and sunlit beams,
Holding secrets, dreams of dreams.
Forever sturdy, ever bright,
The pulse of granite, day and night.

Chronicles Beneath the Archways

Beneath the arches, shadows play,
Whispering stories of yesterday.
Each stone a witness, silent and bold,
Chronicles of ages, waiting to be told.

Light filters through in golden beams,
Caressing past with sunlit dreams.
With every step, the echoes sigh,
Of lives once lived, now gone awry.

Murmurs linger on the stone,
Phantom laughter, never alone.
History dances in every crack,
In archways, never looking back.

Time's embrace won't let them part,
The stories weave, a work of art.
In timeless arches, memories thrive,
Chronicles alive, forever alive.

Silent Guardians of History

Ancient walls, steadfast and true,
Silent guardians that once knew.
They watch the march of fleeting days,
Preserving whispers in their gaze.

Crumbling brick and weathered stone,
Hold the echoes of lives once known.
In every crack, a story lives,
In every shade, a memory gives.

Lifetimes captured in rust and dust,
Every inch a testament of trust.
They stand resolute, resolutely grand,
Silent watchers in every land.

Time may erode, but they remain,
Guardians of joys and silent pain.
Through shadows cast in fading light,
They hold history, day and night.

The Fade of Forgotten Facades

Faded colors, peeling paint,
Whispered dreams, those old complaints.
Windows gazing, lost in thought,
Souvenirs of battles fought.

Once vibrant walls now wear a shroud,
Voices muffle beneath the crowd.
Each step echoes in hollow halls,
Where memory in silence calls.

A tapestry of time unwinds,
In every crack, a truth that binds.
Forgotten stories, tales of grace,
In the fade of their façade's face.

Yet beauty lingers in decay,
A monument to yesterday.
In whispers lost, they still reside,
The fade of facades, time's gentle guide.

Beneath the Crumbling Facade

In shadows deep, where whispers dwell,
The stories fade, the echoes swell.
A broken past in bricks and stone,
In silence lies the truth unknown.

The laughter once, the joy it gift,
Now memories mired in nature's rift.
With every crack, a tale so stark,
The remnants shine, a faded mark.

Beneath the layers of dust and grime,
The heartbeat fades as ghosts unwind.
Each creak and groan, a secret plea,
For eyes to see what used to be.

Yet still the sun will cast its light,
On shattered dreams that feel so right.
And through the ruins, love may bloom,
In crumbling halls, life finds its room.

The Language of Ruins

Words carved in stone, a silent song,
In every fissure, where they belong.
A narrative spun in dust and air,
The language of ruins, whispering rare.

Erosion speaks in gentle sighs,
With every layer, an artist cries.
Memories linger like moths in flight,
Tracing the contours of lost delight.

Time paints its brush with shadows gray,
Telling of lessons in disarray.
The wisdom held in every crack,
Echoes of lives that won't come back.

Yet amidst decay, new stories rise,
In the heart of ruins, hope never dies.
In walls of stone, there lies a truth,
A testament to fleeting youth.

Silhouettes of Silent Towers

Against the dusk, the towers stand,
Guardians of dusk, in silence planned.
Their silhouettes, a haunting sight,
Casting dreams in the fading light.

Their windows dark, hold secrets tight,
Watching the world in endless night.
Each brick a heartbeat, each crack a sigh,
In solitude, beneath the sky.

With every storm, they sway and bend,
But through the ages, they defend.
The whispers of history echo near,
In silent towers, all is clear.

From heights they gaze, on time's cruel flow,
Witness to all—joy, pain, and woe.
In shadows cast by evening's hand,
The figures rise, forever stand.

Ghosts in the Gables

In gable ends, where shadows creep,
The ghosts of yore begin to weep.
With whispers soft, they share their tales,
Of laughter lost in shifting gales.

Once filled with life, each nook and cranny,
Now echoes haunt the air uncanny.
In moonlit nights, they waltz alone,
Recalling joys now overgrown.

Dust dances softly, carried high,
As memories drift and softly sigh.
Through cracks in wood, they seek a way,
To linger on till light of day.

Yet in their sorrow, there is grace,
A timeless love can't be erased.
In gables worn, they find their peace,
Little by little, they release.

Echos of Sacred Spaces

Whispers of the ancients dwell,
In shadows where the spirits fell.
Each stone a story, each sigh a prayer,
In sacred spaces, secrets rare.

Moonlit pathways, soft and bright,
Guide the wandering souls at night.
Echoes linger, timeless and clear,
Embracing hearts that wander near.

Amidst the trees, the silence speaks,
In rustling leaves, the wisdom seeks.
A gentle breeze, a call to hear,
The sacred places draw us near.

In every step, a heartbeat's trace,
In every breath, a sacred grace.
We gather here, both near and far,
In echos of these spaces, we are.

Dreams Shaped by the Ancients

In twilight's glow, shadows dance,
We weave our dreams in sacred trance.
Through whispered tales of times long gone,
Ancient wisdom guides us on.

The stars above, a cosmic map,
Charting paths where dreams can nap.
With every wish, a story spun,
In the fabric of all, we're one.

Time flows like a river wide,
Carrying hopes on its gentle tide.
Through ancient eyes, we find our way,
To futures bright, in night's ballet.

Voices echo from the past,
In timeless dreams, our hopes are cast.
Together we rise, together we roam,
In dreams shaped by the ancients, we find our home.

Etched Tomorrows in Brick

Walls rise high, ambitions stark,
Each brick a dream, each line a mark.
Stories nestled in mortar and clay,
Etched tomorrows guide our way.

Underneath the sun's warm glow,
Foundations laid, aspirations grow.
A legacy of toil and sweat,
In every corner, dreams are met.

Hand in hand, we build and dream,
A tapestry woven, a vibrant seam.
Brick by brick, we forge the path,
Creating futures beyond the math.

Echoes of laughter, whispers of pain,
In every space, the loss and gain.
Together we rise, in unity we stick,
Etched tomorrows, crafted in brick.

Conversations with the Cornice

Above the hustle, where silence lies,
The cornice holds the whispered skies.
Its curves and edges, tales untold,
Of moments cherished, of dreams bold.

Glimmers catch the evening light,
Conversations dance from day to night.
In shadows cast, reflections swirl,
As stories of life in beauty unfurl.

Each detail whispers, soft yet clear,
A history felt through every year.
Loyal witness to joy and strife,
The cornice cradles the essence of life.

So pause awhile, in this embrace,
And listen close to time and space.
For in these corners, we find our way,
In conversations with the cornice, we stay.

Canvas of Timeworn Structures

Through crumbling walls, stories unfold,
Whispers of history, silent yet bold.
Brick by brick, the tales intertwine,
In each crevice, memories shine.

Windows shattered, dreams once bright,
Fragments embrace the fading light.
Nature's brush paints the decay,
An artist's touch, a soft ballet.

Rust and ivy, the colors of age,
Past echoes dance upon the stage.
Each layer thick with time's embrace,
In this canvas, we find our place.

The heartbeat of the earth's own skin,
An art form where life begins.
In every fold, the past resides,
A tapestry where history hides.

Melodies of Marble and Mortar

Chisels sing on stone so grand,
Melodies whisper, a timeless band.
Each blow resonates with grace,
Carving dreams in a sacred space.

Fluted columns reach for the skies,
Echoes of laughter in stone replies.
Mortar binds what time can't sever,
A harmony that lasts forever.

On polished floors, shadows sway,
Step by step, they dance and play.
Voices linger in every hall,
A serenade that won't let fall.

In arches high, where silence sings,
The heartbeats of forgotten kings.
In the stillness, echoes found,
Melodies of marble, profound.

The Lament of Lost Landscapes

Whispers of fields, once lush and wide,
Now fading dreams where memories bide.
Mountains, shadows of days long past,
Their majesty, a shadow cast.

Rivers dry, their songs suppressed,
Echoes of life, in stillness dressed.
The wind carries notes of sorrow,
A lament for an unseen tomorrow.

Trees stand gaunt, stripped of their cloak,
Nature's breath, a wistful choke.
The skies weep, a heavy gray,
For the landscapes lost along the way.

In every corner, silence reigns,
A requiem for the forgotten plains.
Yet deep within, a seed remains,
Hope for renewal in the chains.

Chimeras in the Masonry

In the heart of stone, creatures dwell,
Mosaic dreams, a silent spell.
Eyes of glass and laughter bright,
Chimeras dance in the pale moonlight.

Wings of shadow stretch and soar,
Fables etched in the brick and floor.
Whispers echo through ancient halls,
The spirit of wonder breathes and calls.

Faces form in a tangle of vines,
Guardians of the past, where history shines.
Each crack a portal, each seam a guide,
In the masonry, lost worlds abide.

What lies beneath the stony facade?
Mysteries woven, both rare and odd.
The chimeras beckon us to see,
Life is carved within the debris.

The Echoing Silence of Stonework

In shadows cast by ancient stone,
Whispers linger, soft and lone.
Time stands still, a quiet breath,
Echoing secrets of life and death.

The cold embrace of weathered walls,
Holds the tales of distant calls.
Nature's grip, a gentle hand,
Cradles history across the land.

Under arches, silence blooms,
In hallowed halls, a silence looms.
Footsteps fade on paths well-trod,
Marking places, where echoes nod.

Yet in the quiet, voices rise,
Carried softly through the skies.
Stone may rest but will not sleep,
In silence, memories weep.

Haunting Harmonies in Helices

In spiraled forms, the echoes tread,
Harmonies within the threads are wed.
Whirling notes and shadows play,
In winding paths, they dance and sway.

Softly sung, the spirals hum,
Calling forth the dreams to come.
Every twist, a tale entwined,
In each curve, a thought defined.

From whispers borne on gentle air,
The haunting tunes beyond compare.
Resonance in the muted night,
Guides lost souls to find the light.

In every spiral, truth unveils,
Harmonious streams like silver trails.
Woven deep in spirals, grace,
Time retreats, in this sacred space.

Timelessness Through the Threshold

A doorway stands, a passage low,
Where time suspends its steady flow.
Crossing over, worlds collide,
In that space, dreams safely hide.

The threshold glimmers, softly beams,
A portal woven of hopes and dreams.
Each step taken, moments freeze,
In this realm where hearts find ease.

Endless echoes through the frame,
Resonate with whispered names.
Beyond the threshold, time's embrace,
Awaits the wanderer's soft trace.

Each heartbeat marks a silent beat,
In timelessness, we feel complete.
Through the door, the past we find,
In every promise, love aligned.

Woven Whispers in the Weald

In the weald where the wild things roam,
Nature sings a harmonic poem.
Whispers woven through the trees,
Carried softly on the breeze.

Each leaf a tale, each branch a song,
In the forest where we belong.
Among the roots, secrets lie,
Beneath the watchful, open sky.

From the undergrowth, echoes rise,
Spirits dance, the ground replies.
Woven threads of light and shade,
In shadows deep, our dreams are laid.

In this realm, where whispers dwell,
The weald is alive, a living shell.
Nature's chorus, a gentle bind,
In every breath, the heart entwined.

Ghosts of the Gabled Roof

In shadows cast by old pine trees,
Whispers float on the evening breeze.
Echoes of laughter from days gone by,
Ghosts roam free beneath the sky.

Windows cracked, stories untold,
Fragments of memories, brave and bold.
The gabled roof, a sentinel still,
Holds secrets deep against its will.

Misty nights with a soft caress,
Bring wandering souls to find their rest.
Through silent halls and dusty rooms,
They dance alone amidst the glooms.

Gather ye round, as shadows blend,
Where time stands still and dreams don't end.
For in the corners, where silence sleeps,
The heart of the house forever keeps.

The Language of the Lost

Words unspoken like autumn leaves,
Drifting softly on the evening eaves.
Echoes linger in the twilight's glow,
A language spoken where no one goes.

In the spaces between heartbeats,
Silent stories, the soul retreats.
Gestures made in the shadows cast,
Resonate softly, a flickering past.

Wandering thoughts in a whispered breeze,
Sway like branches on ancient trees.
The language of lost, a tender thread,
Connects the living with the dead.

Listen closely to the night's embrace,
For in the silence, we find our place.
Unraveling time, as stars align,
In forgotten tongues, our dreams entwine.

Imprints of the Unseen

Beneath the surface where shadows play,
Imprints linger of a brighter day.
Threads of thought woven through air,
Whispers of moments that vanish bare.

Each footprint tells a tale so grand,
Stories written in grains of sand.
Hidden truths beneath our feet,
In every crack, a life complete.

Time leaves echoes on the stone,
Memories etched, never alone.
In each heartbeat, a silent scream,
Imprints of lives, like a forgotten dream.

So tread lightly where spirits roam,
For the unseen makes this place home.
In the quiet, feel the past's embrace,
In imprints of love, we find our space.

Secrets Embedded in Brick

Walls stand tall, sturdy and proud,
Whispering secrets beneath the shroud.
Each brick laid with a story to tell,
Of lives entwined in a timeless spell.

Cracks form lines like rivers run deep,
Hiding tales that the night would keep.
Worn edges speak of laughter and tears,
In every corner, the weight of years.

Covered with ivy, their tales unfold,
Like ancient scrolls from the days of old.
A fortress of whispers, memories entwined,
In shadows of brick, the past we find.

So walk these paths where echoes dwell,
Each step a note in a living cell.
For secrets buried in time's embrace,
Live on in brick, a sacred space.

Songs of the Static Structure

In shadows cast by towering stone,
The songs of silence find their tone.
Each corner holds a whispered tale,
As echoes linger, never pale.

Grit and grace in every crack,
Time's embrace cannot hold back.
The walls may wear, yet dreams remain,
In memories held, a soft refrain.

With every breath, the past awakes,
In dreams of lives that time forsakes.
Within the stillness, voices rise,
To pierce the firmament of skies.

So listen close, let heartbeams trace,
The pulse of life in every space.
A symphony of souls in thrall,
In static structures, we hear the call.

Where History Hums Beneath

Upon the soil where stories grow,
The whispers of the ancients flow.
Footprints linger in the earth,
Each marking tales of joy and mirth.

In every rustle, a song persists,
Where dreams collide with history's mist.
A tapestry woven from hope and strife,
In every heart, the pulse of life.

With every heartbeat, shadows dance,
In pain and love, a timeless trance.
In echoes soft, the lessons teach,
Of longing hearts, within our reach.

Awake, the dreams of those who came,
In whispered past, we find our name.
Where history hums, we stand and breathe,
A legacy in roots, we weave.

Whispers on Wind-Swept Walkways

Through cobbled streets where breezes sigh,
Whispers linger beneath the sky.
With every step, the stories glide,
In twilight's embrace, memories bide.

The trees would sway, their branches share,
Secrets carried in fragrant air.
In shadows cast by fleeting light,
Ghostly figures whisper, take flight.

With every gust, the tales unfold,
Of lovers lost and heroes bold.
In every corner, a flickering soul,
A journey shared, a search for whole.

So wander freely, hearts unchained,
Let wanderlust guide, never restrained.
For on these walkways, dreams entwine,
In whispers soft, the stars align.

Cascades of Forgotten Design

Echoes of water, softly flow,
Whispers of beauty, gone long ago.
Shapes in the mist, memories entwined,
Lost in the stream, what once was defined.

Fading reflections, shimmer and fade,
Hiding the stories, time never made.
Nature's embrace, a gentle reprieve,
In cascades of silence, past dreams weave.

Carved in the stone, the touch of the rain,
Bridges to moments, joy and to pain.
Time's silent witness, it holds within,
The cascades of life, where all must begin.

In tranquil descent, the waters confide,
Tales of the ages, in ripples they hide.
Cascades of memory, flowing so free,
A dance of forgotten, now part of the sea.

Crafted Corners of Collapse

In shadows they linger, the corners so tight,
Crafted with care, now fading from sight.
Lines once so sharp, now softened by time,
Revisiting places where echoes still chime.

Walls built of promise, now wearing so thin,
Bound by the memories, lost deep within.
In whispers they crumble, the stories unfold,
Crafted with wisdom, now tales of the old.

Haunted by laughter that once filled the halls,
Now silence reigns where the heart seldom calls.
Corners of dreams, once vibrant and grand,
Now crafted in shadows, too frail to withstand.

Yet hope lingers softly, a thread in the night,
In crafted collapse, there's still a soft light.
A testament woven with each fragile breath,
In corners of loss, there's beauty in depth.

Layers of Lore in the Walls

Ancient inscriptions, whispers of yore,
Carved in the timber, secrets restore.
Layers of stories, each year that has passed,
Walls hold the echoes, too precious to last.

Tales of the hearth, where fires burned bright,
Guardians of dreams, through day and through night.
In every chipped surface, a memory lies,
Layers of lore, in the silence they rise.

Colors of life, painted with grace,
Fade over seasons, but time can't erase.
Fragments of laughter, and whispers of woe,
In layers of age, their essence will grow.

In shadows they linger, entwined in the frame,
Layers of lore, in the heart, they reclaim.
Among these walls, history sings,
In every soft murmur, the past softly clings.

Silenced Sagas of Structure

In the rustling leaves, where sunlight will dance,
Silenced sagas wait, for a moment's chance.
Cracked bricks and mortar, they whisper their tales,
Of grandeur and sorrow, where history pales.

Echoing footsteps through corridors wide,
Stories unspoken in silence abide.
Fragments of laughter, long lost in the air,
Silenced sagas dwell, in the shadows they share.

Time stands as witness to every small crack,
Each flaw a reminder, there's no turning back.
In the breath of the night, as whispers converge,
Silenced sagas of structure, in silence emerge.

With each passing season, the layers unfold,
In the heart of the building, the tales to be told.
From foundations to rooftops, the spirit awakes,
In silenced sagas, the past gently shakes.

Harmonies Held by Handrails

In whispers soft, the metal bends,
Embracing dreams that time defends.
With every step, a tale unfolds,
In silent notes, the journey holds.

Along the path, we share our grace,
Hand in hand, we find our place.
The echoes of our laughter rise,
As we traverse the starry skies.

Safety's clasp, a gentle guide,
Where hearts align and hopes abide.
Through shadowed halls, our spirits soar,
In unity, we seek for more.

Together here, as night descends,
In harmony, our love transcends.
With each embrace, the world feels bright,
Held by handrails, we share the light.

Foundations of Forgotten Futures

In crumbling walls, a story lies,
Whispers of dreams that touch the skies.
Forgotten hopes in dust reside,
Yet courage grows, no need to hide.

Each brick a memory, strong and true,
Foundations built from me and you.
Through time's embrace, our lives entwine,
In roots we find a sacred sign.

The blueprints drawn in hearts of flame,
Ignite the past, call out our name.
From often lost, we shall arise,
To claim the dawn, to touch the skies.

With every step, we forge anew,
Forgotten paths, our spirits true.
In futures bright, our tales will soar,
As we reclaim what was before.

Celestial Connections of the Built

Under the stars, the structures gleam,
Concrete dreams in silver beam.
Connections forged in twilight's breath,
Beneath the vast, we conquer death.

Skyscrapers rise, like hands that reach,
Embracing hope with lessons teach.
In every beam, a story skies,
Celestial whispers, where love lies.

Through every arch, the cosmos see,
In bridges built, we're wild and free.
Networks formed in shadow and light,
Celestial bonds that shine so bright.

In structures grand, our dreams entwine,
In whispered tales, our hearts align.
Together we, the stars embrace,
In every space, we find our place.

Layers of Light in Lintels

Upon the frame, the light spills down,
In glowing hues, the edges drown.
Each layer tells of days gone by,
In gentle folds, beneath the sky.

The sunbeam dances, shadows play,
In every corner, night meets day.
Across the lintels, soft and warm,
A tapestry of calm and storm.

The weight of time rests on the beams,
In whispered light, we weave our dreams.
With every layer, our story grows,
In hidden depths, our love bestows.

Through all the trials, love brings the gold,
As layers shift, our souls unfold.
In light we see, forever binds,
In gentle beams, our heart aligns.

Eclipsed by Time

Shadows dance beneath the starry night,
Memories fade with the morning light.
Each tick, a whisper of moments lost,
We chase what was, ignoring the cost.

Fleeting echoes of voices unclear,
In the silence, we hold what we fear.
Brush of history paints on our skin,
In the shadows, we search for the sin.

Time's hand slips, a thief in twilight,
Glimmers of gold in the fading sight.
Life's kaleidoscope spins without stop,
Eclipsed by time, we rise and we drop.

Frayed at the Edges

Threads of existence pulled ever tight,
Fading borders in the soft dusk light.
A heart worn thin by moments of strain,
Each stitch a story, joy with the pain.

Worn-out pages of a life well-read,
Turning softly, the chapters misled.
Fingers trace tales of laughter and tears,
Whispers of hope mixed with flickers of fears.

In the seams, a fabric of dreams sewn,
Frayed at the edges, yet never alone.
We gather the pieces, create from the torn,
In our fragility, strength is reborn.

Visions from the Vaulted Ceilings

Under arches where secrets reside,
Whispers of angels begin to collide.
Colors of stained glass spark the divine,
In shadows and light, our souls intertwine.

Dreams painted high on the vaulted space,
Each vision breathes life into empty face.
Silent conspiracies held in the air,
In the stillness, our hopes lay bare.

Caught in the glow of transcendent grace,
We trace the lines of a celestial place.
In silence, we linger and feel the allure,
Visions from ceilings, forever secure.

The Lure of Lingering Luminance

A glow lingers on the edge of the night,
Fleeting moments wrapped in soft light.
Stars beckon with whispers of dreams,
In their dance, we find hidden themes.

Radiance weaving through silken air,
Promises whispered, secrets to share.
The moon's smile ignites our delight,
Glowing softly, a beacon of light.

Life's shadows retreat in the gleaming warm,
The lure of luminance breaks every norm.
We follow the spark, hearts open wide,
Chasing the shades where the light does abide.

A Palimpsest of Places

Layered landscapes etched in our minds,
Footsteps resonate where memory binds.
Maps of our journeys sketch every line,
Through the echoes, the past intertwines.

Cities of wonder, hills of despair,
Each stone remembers the hearts laid bare.
In the murmurs of streets, we hear the call,
A palimpsest written for one and for all.

Faded inscriptions of joy and of pain,
History breathes through the sun and the rain.
With every revisit, new stories emerge,
In every detail, our lives converge.

Whispers of Stone

In the quiet of the night, unseen,
Lies the tale that once had been.
Echoes of laughter, whispers of pain,
Carried on winds, like a soft refrain.

Each crack and crevice holds a dream,
Held in silence, like a beam.
Time stands still in the muted light,
Where stories linger, out of sight.

The moss grows thick, the shadows creep,
Guarding secrets that they keep.
A world beneath, ancient and bold,
In each pebble, a memory told.

So listen close, the stones will speak,
Of hearts once strong, now frail and weak.
In every whisper, a legacy shines,
In the heart of the earth, history binds.

Shadows in the Archways

Beneath the arches, shadows dance,
In hues of twilight, lost in trance.
Whispers of lovers, stories unfold,
Etched in silence, memories bold.

The light filters through, casting gloom,
Each shadow holds a hint of doom.
Yet in the darkness, beauty blooms,
In the silence that softly looms.

Ghosts of laughter linger near,
Echoes of joy, mingled with fear.
Time's passage marks the stones with grace,
Shadows embrace, a timeless trace.

So linger longer, in this place,
Where history breathes with quiet grace.
Through every arch, a tale to find,
Shadows entwined with the winds of time.

Fragments of Forgotten Walls

Crumbled bricks tell tales untold,
Walls that stood, now worn and old.
Each fragment whispers of days gone by,
In the cracks, a silent sigh.

Lost voices echo in the stone,
Fragments of dreams, forever lone.
Life once thrived in every crevice,
Now memories lie in a fragile bliss.

Painted layers, colors fade,
Stories woven, serenely laid.
What once was vibrant, now subdued,
In the silence, a solemn mood.

Yet hope lingers in the dust,
In the ruins, a quiet trust.
For even walls, though broken, stand,
Holding fragments of a distant land.

Reverberations of the Past

In the corridors of time, we tread,
Where echoes of history softly spread.
Each step resounds, a haunting call,
Reverberations from walls that fall.

The air is thick with whispered lore,
Tales of triumph, battles, and more.
Voices linger like an ancient hymn,
Resounding softly, on the limb.

Through shadows cast and light so frail,
The past weaves in a tender tale.
What once resounded, now a sigh,
Yet still it breathes, never to die.

So pause a moment, heed the sound,
In every heartbeat, the lost is found.
For in the echoes, life can be seen,
Reverberations of what has been.